2022
BUENOS AIRES
Restaurants

The Food Enthusiast's
Long Weekend Guide

Andrew Delaplaine

Andrew Delaplaine *is the Food Enthusiast.*
When he's not playing tennis,
he dines anonymously at the Publisher's (considerable)
expense.

James Cubby – Senior Editor

The Food Enthusiast's Long Weekend Guide

Table of Contents

Introduction

What a fascinating country. You walk down the avenues of BA and look at some of the well-heeled ladies and gentlemen promenading and you'd never know the country is always on the brink of some new disaster (usually self-inflicted), whether it's a debt crisis, or a political scandal involving some important person's assassination. Whatever it is, it's always something.

But somehow BA not only endures, it thrives. There's a sophistication about the people here that manages to transcend the ephemeral problems that besiege the country as a whole.

It's always reminded me of Marseille, that other polyglot of a town. In Marseille, because it was such a centrally located trading port, there's the confluence of cultural influences that go back 3,000 years—all surging together in that remarkable city.

Here in BA, the Romans never landed and the Carthaginians never tramped through on their elephants, but still BA has an impressive mixture of cultural elements from France, Spain, Portugal, Italy—everywhere, really.

These bedazzling influences have combined to create a vibrant dining scene that has become even more impressive in the last few years.

Get ready for an onslaught of meat-based dishes. The Atkins diet on steroids. Nobody handles meat the way these guys do. (That reminds me of something Sarah Palin said: "If God hadn't wanted us to eat animals, He wouldn't have made them out of meat.")

So, between your tango lessons and visits to what has to be one of the most interesting cemeteries in the world (the Recoleta), spend as much time as you can in the eateries of Buenos Aires.

You will agree with native son Jorge Luis Borges, that, "To me, it seems a mere tale that

Buenos Aires had a beginning: I judge her to be as
eternal as water and air."

A WORD ABOUT MONEY
The official exchange rate is a joke, so both
locals and tourists have turned to the black market to
get what they call "blue dollars." *Arbolitos* are street
hawkers who help you get these blue dollars. You
will hear them yelling "Cambio!" Hook up with one
of them and they will take you to *Cuevas* that sell
currency. A site giving you the current rate is
www.lanacion.com -- this can save you a lot of
money.

The
A to Z
Listings

Ridiculously Extravagant
Sensible Alternatives
Quality Bargain Spots

A note on the **Puertas Cerradas** (or "closed door" restaurants) that abound in BA. They don't like to give out their addresses as a rule until you get a reservation from them. Try emailing first, then calling. Much better if you get someone who speaks Spanish to do it for you. But these are great spots and very much worth the effort.)

ACONCAGUA

Bolívar 905, Buenos Aires, +54 11 4362-3826
CUISINE: Argentinean
DRINKS: Full bar
SERVING: Breakfast, Lunch & Dinner; closed Sun
PRICE RANGE: $
NEIGHBORHOOD: San Telmo
A classic old bar located in a quiet corner of San
Telmo populated by locals. Great menu of homemade
cuisine, all cooked when you order it. They have
daily set menus, and this is what you want to try.
Open 24 hours a day. On Sundays the locals gather to
watch sports.

ALDO'S VINOTECA

Moreno 372 Caba, Buenos Aires, 54 11 4334-2380
www.aldosvinoteca.com
CUISINE: Argentinean

DRINKS: Full Bar
SERVING: Breakfast, Brunch, Late night
PRICE RANGE: $$
NEIGHBORHOOD: Monserrat; San Telmo
Located in the heart of the city in the **Moreno Hotel,** this restaurant offers and elegant dining experience. Nice menu and perhaps the most impressive wine list in town (over 40 pages) with mostly Argentine wines but some Spanish and Italian labels. Nice choice for Sunday brunch.

ALO'S
Blanco Encalada 2120, Buenos Aires, +54 11 4737-0248
https://www.facebook.com/AlosBistro/
CUISINE: French/Argentinean/Vegetarian Friendly
DRINKS: Full Bar
SERVING: Breakfast, Lunch & Dinner; Closed Sun

PRICE RANGE: $$$
NEIGHBORHOOD: Boulogne
Out in the suburb of San Isidro is this 5-star rated
upscale eatery designed like a modern bistro offering
casual Argentinean cuisine with a 7-course tasting
menu. The trick they pull off here is taking traditional
Argentine flavors and somehow mixing them up into
something extraordinary. A wine expert comes to
your table to assist you in wine choices. Creative
desserts come from a very talented pastry chef.
Reservations recommended.

ANAFE
Virrey Avilés 3216, Buenos Aires, +54 11 5634-1978
https://www.instagram.com/anafe.ba/
CUISINE: Healthy/Vegetarian Friendly/Gluten Free
Options
DRINKS: Full Bar
SERVING: Lunch & Dinner
PRICE RANGE: $$$$
NEIGHBORHOOD: Colegiales
Upscale "health" eatery serving tapas style dishes.
Favorites: Ricotta with chapati and Pork
Churrasquito. Delicious desserts. Reservations
recommended.

ANCHOITA

Juan Ramírez de Velasco 1520, Buenos Aires, +54 11 4854-9334

https://anchoita.meitre.com/

CUISINE: Argentine

DRINKS: Full Bar

SERVING: Dinner; Closed Sun

PRICE RANGE: $$$

NEIGHBORHOOD: Chacarita

Unique eatery offering an upscale dining experience serving Argentine favorites. The wooden bar wraps around the kitchen so you can see all the wonderful dishes they create here—from the crudos, to the pasta, to the river fishes expertly prepared, down to the high quality cheeses. They book well in advance, so if you want to take in this spot, plan ahead. You won't regret it. (However, I've lucked out and been able to walk in on occasion during a week night.) Impressive wine selection.

ARAMBURU

Pasaje del Correo, Vicente López 1661, Buenos
Aires, +54 11 4811 1414
www.arambururesto.com.ar
CUISINE: Argentinian/International
DRINKS: Full Bar
SERVING: Dinner
PRICE RANGE: $$$$
NEIGHBORHOOD: Constitucion
Raw brick walls greet you as you enter. The eye drifts
to the clear glass window that lets you look into the
kitchen. Known as one of the top five restaurants in
Buenos Aires and like most of the finer restaurants a
reservation is a must. The menu is in courses (last
time I was there we had 16 courses all paired with
wine for less than $100) but they offer many delicious
dishes like White Salmon and Filet Mignon. Great
selection of wines. If they are jammed (and they
usually are), opt for the less formal place across the
street, **Aramburu Bis**, owned by the same chef. After
dinner, check out the bar downstairs in the basement.

CAFÉ LA BIELA

Avenida Quintana 600, Buenos Aires, 54 11 4804-
0449
www.labiela.com
CUISINE: Cafeteria
DRINKS: Full Bar
SERVING: Lunch, Dinner
PRICE RANGE: $$$
NEIGHBORHOOD: Recoleta
This traditional Argentine café, originally a meeting
place for racecar drivers, is one of the oldest cafés in

BA, going back 150 years. You'll see the walls inside this place lined with racecar memorabilia, lots of photos of famous drivers—most now long dead—look down from the walls. Though it's a bit of a tourist trap in the way Sloppy Joe's is in Key West, it's still worth visiting. I prefer inside where you get the dark wood paneling, the ceiling fans and the charm. I don't fancy the plastic chairs outside, but in good weather it's a really nice spot. Extensive menu

serving large portions. Jorge Luis Borges, probab;ly the m,ost famous writer NOT awarded the Nobel Prize, lived just a short walk from here, and used to visit often.

CAFÉ SAN JUAN
Chile 474, Buenos Aires, 54 11 4300-9344
No Website
CUISINE: Italian/Spanish
DRINKS: Full Bar
SERVING: Breakfast, Lunch, Dinner
PRICE RANGE: $
NEIGHBORHOOD: San Telmo
This tiny place is popular with locals and tourists, this small restaurant (the kitchen is in full view where you can see the owner slaving away cooking his meat-centric dishes) offers a menu with a distinct Argentine influence. Try the rabbit stew, it's a favorite.

CANTINA PIERINO
Lavalle 3499, Buenos Aires, 54 11-4864-5715
No Website
CUISINE: Italian
DRINKS: Full Bar
SERVING: Lunch, Dinner

PRICE RANGE: $$$
NEIGHBORHOOD: Almagro
If you don't want to learn the tango, the next best thing is to come to this Italian-style cantina because it's filled with loads of tango memorabilia. The food is homemade Italian cuisine. Actually, there's really not a menu, they just bring you food and everything is cooked fresh. This place is always packed.

Casa Cavia

CASA CAVIA

Cavia 2985, Buenos Aires, +54 11 4809-8600
https://casacavia.com/
CUISINE: Eclectic/Fusion/Argentinean
DRINKS: Full Bar
SERVING: Lunch & Dinner
PRICE RANGE: $$$$
NEIGHBORHOOD: Palermo
Upscale Argentinean eatery with a creative menu set
in a beautiful old house that shares space with
publishing house, a stylish bar (where you can have a
drink before going into the restaurant), a flower shop
and a whole lot more, creating quite an interesting
buzz. When there's no rush, try to spend a lazy
afternoon out in the garden. Menu picks: Avocado
salad with grilled trout and Beef ribs with chimichurri
sauce. Impressive wine selection.

CASA FELIX

Address given with reservation, 54 9 11 4555-1882
www.colectivofelix.com

CUISINE: Argentinean
DRINKS: Full Bar
SERVING: Dinner
PRICE RANGE: $$$$
NEIGHBORHOOD: El Centro
Closed Door Restaurant. This place only seats 12 guests for a private five-course tasting menu three times a week. Menu changes with each seating but the dishes are creative and tasty. Long wait for reservations.

CHAN CHAN

Hipolito Yrigoyen 1390, Buenos Aires, 54 11 4382-8492
https://chanchanbsas.business.site
CUISINE: Peruvian
DRINKS: Full bar
SERVING: Lunch & Dinner; Dinner only on Sat
PRICE RANGE: $$
NEIGHBORHOOD: Congreso
Great place to go to experience Peruvian cuisine at a budget price. People crowd in here during the lunch hour packed tight as sardines, chowing down on plates of ceviche, ajiaco de conejo (rabbit stew), arroz chaufa (fried rice Peruvian style), Creamy Chicken and Cheese stuffed fish. My advice is to wash it all down with an excellent Peruvian beer.

CHILA

Alicia Moreau de Justo 1160, Buenos Aires, +54 11 4343-6067
www.chilaweb.com.ar
CUISINE: Modern Argentinean

DRINKS: Full bar
SERVING: Dinner; closed Mon
PRICE RANGE: $$$$
NEIGHBORHOOD: Puerto Madero
Argentinean cuisine served a la carte or from the pre-fix menu. The chef studied in
Spain, so there are some interesting twists on local dishes. Also, you can find non-traditional dishes served including: Quail, quinoa and sucking pig. Unlike a lot of restaurants here, seafood is emphasized. Nice wine selection.

CHORI
Thames 1653, Buenos Aires, +54 11 3966-9857
www.facebook.com/Xchorix/

CUISINE: Steakhouse/Argentinean
DRINKS: Full Bar
SERVING: Lunch & Dinner; closed Mondays
PRICE RANGE: $
NEIGHBORHOOD: Palermo
Perfect place for Choripan (chorizo on bread). This place treats the humble sandwich like a king, and produces a gourmet version of it. Favorites: Colorado Picate and Smoked Pork. Great selection of artisanal beers and classic tonic drinks.

CORTE COMEDOR
Av. Olazábal 1391, C1428 C1428ASK, Buenos Aires, +54 11 4781-2166
https://corte-comedor.meitre.com/
CUISINE: Barbecue/Argentinean/Gluten Free Options
DRINKS: Full Bar
SERVING: Breakfast, Lunch & Dinner; Breakfast & Lunch only on Sun
PRICE RANGE: $$$
NEIGHBORHOOD: Belgrano
Argentinean Steakhouse offering an assorted menu of meats. Favorites: Tomahawk steak and the Chorizo (lamb, rabbit, morcilla and chistorra). Delicious desserts. Reservations recommended.

CROQUE MADAME
NATIONAL MUSEUM OF DECORATIVE ART
Av Callao 1569, Buenos Aires, 54 11 4812-0777
www.croquemadame.com.ar
CUISINE: Tea Room/Coffee Shop
DRINKS: Beer & Wine

SERVING: Lunch, Dinner
PRICE RANGE: $$$$
NEIGHBORHOOD: Palermo
Located in the Museum of Decorative Art, this

café/restaurant is a great stop for an afternoon snack
or coffee after touring the museum. (I stop in the
morning for café con leche before touring the
museum—get the homemade scones.) It's actually
out in a courtyard where you'll love the sound of the
wind rustling through the tall shade trees and listen to
the splashing fountains. Menu offers a variety of
sandwiches, pizzas, pastas and sweet treats, and of
course the signature Croques.

CUERVO CAFÉ
El Salvador 4580, Buenos Aires, +54 11 4149-7509
http://www.cuervocafe.com/

CUISINE: Cafe
DRINKS: No Booze
SERVING: Lunch & Dinner
PRICE RANGE: $$
NEIGHBORHOOD: Palermo
Café serving avocado toasts, sandwiches, cinnamon rolls, croissants, and coffees.

CUMANA

Rodriguez Pena 1149, Buenos Aires, +54 11 4813-9207

www.cumanahorno.com.ar/

 CUISINE: Argentine, Tapas/Small Plates, Pizza
DRINKS: Beer & Wine Only
SERVING: Lunch & Dinner
PRICE RANGE: $$
NEIGHBORHOOD: Recoleta
You probably haven't seen an adobe oven before, but they have one here. Large windows let the light flow in during the day. A great budget place. Taste some of the delicious authentic Argentinean (regional) cuisine including empanadas, pizzas (different that American pizza) and stews. Go for a *cazuela,* which is essentially a stew of corn, eggplant, potatoes, squash and meat. Bursting with flavor. Welcoming to tourists but it's essentially a locals' eatery.

DON JULIO

Guatemala 4691, Buenos Aires, +54 11 4831-9564
www.parrilladonjulia.com.ar
WEBSITE DOWN AT PRESSTIME
CUISINE: Steakhouse
DRINKS: Beer & Wine Only

SERVING: Lunch & Dinner
PRICE RANGE: $$$
Rustic steakhouse with a costumed maître d' greeting guests. He will seat you at a table covered with a leather tablecloth (each one the hide of a whole cow). Great place for meat lovers with an extensive wine list. Try the grilled provolone with tomato as an appetizer and you can't go wrong ordering one of their steaks. But instead of the usual sirloin, tenderloin or delicious skirt steak, I'd try their sweetbreads, delectable morsels expertly prepared. Or their kidneys and chitlins as a starter. Seating upstairs and down.

EL BAQUEANO
Chile 499, Buenos Aires, +54 11 4342-0802
www.restoelbaqueano.com
CUISINE: Argentinean
DRINKS: Full Bar
SERVING: Dinner; closed Sun & Mon

PRICE RANGE: $$$$
NEIGHBORHOOD: Monserrat
A unique restaurant as it only serves local game meat
– everything from Lama to fish. Nice wine pairings.
Great tasting menu.

EL FERROVIARIO

Reservistas Argentinos 219, +54 11 4643-9164
https://elferroviarioparrilla.com/
CUISINE: Argentine / steakhouse
DRINKS: Beer & Wine Only
SERVING: Lunch & Dinner
PRICE RANGE: $$
NEIGHBORHOOD: Liniers
Great menu offering everything from squid to all
kinds of meat, as befitting a "popular," which is the
Argentine word for steakhouse. Wonderfully rustic
and charming atmosphere with clusters of garlic

hanging from the wood-beamed cathedral ceiling
along with sides of cured ham, cheeses, etc. Big
tables are meant to seat families or a group of friends,
so a crowd is welcome. (There's a tent outside for the
overflow crowd.) This used to be the cafeteria for the
Liniers football stadium. Favorites: parrillada, or
mixed grill, which includes everything from
sweetbreads, chorizo, proveleta, large cuts of
succulent and aroma rich meat ready to fall from the
bone. Nice selection of desserts including an
incredible flan.

EL MIRASOL DAL PUERTO
Av. Alicia Moreau de Justo 202, +54 11 4315-6277
www.elmirasol.com.ar
CUISINE: Steakhouse
DRINKS: Full Bar
SERVING: Lunch & Dinner
PRICE RANGE: $$$
NEIGHBORHOOD: Puerto Madero
Nice eatery (the name of this place means "the
sunflower of the port") with English speaking waiters
that help you navigate the menu in this lovely spot
that overlooks the sparkling yachts docked outside.
Beside the quay you're surrounded by soaring office
towers, but here it's very quaint for a power lunch
place that attracts well-heeled business types.
Favorites: just throw caution and calories to the wind
and indulge in the meats on offer here—the 1.5 pound
cut is ordered by more people than you'd think, but
you can get a simple 1-pound steak if you like. If you
order a whole chorizo, be prepared to share it. The

Salmon empanadas are well worth sampling. Note: there is a minimal "per person" charge.

EL POBRE LUIS

Arribeños 2393, Buenos Aires, 11-4780-5847
CUISINE: Argentinian
DRINKS: Full Bar
SERVING: Lunch, Dinner
PRICE RANGE: $$$$
NEIGHBORHOOD: Capital Federal

A favorite restaurant among the locals for their house specialty, Pamplona – Beef, Chicken or Pork rolled with ham, cheese and red peppers and then grilled. Still, I prefer the veal sweetbreads or the ojo de bife (rib eye). This place has an open parrilla (grill), making it easy to watch the cooks slinging all that meat around. A great spectacle. (Closed Sundays).

EL PREFERIDO DE PALERMO

Jorge Luis Borges 2108, Buenos Aires, +54 11 4774-6585
No Website
CUISINE: Argentinean
DRINKS: Full Bar
SERVING: Lunch & Dinner; closed Sun
PRICE RANGE: $$
NEIGHBORHOOD: Palermo
This place looks like a small old market but it's a great choice for snacks and drinks. Not a touristy stop – locals only. Favorites: Tripe stew (a starter) and Veal ribs with salad. Most dishes are cooked home style. Don't leave without trying the flan with dulce de leche for dessert.

ELENA

Posadas 1086, Buenos Aires, +54 11 4321-1200

https://www.fourseasons.com/buenosaires
CUISINE: Argentine
DRINKS: Full bar
SERVING: Breakfast, Lunch & Dinner
PRICE RANGE: $$$$
NEIGHBORHOOD: Retiro
Chic restaurant located in the **Four Seasons Hotel**, offering fine dining experience. It's one of those places you go for a special occasion like a birthday because it's no nice, with great service and high prices. (Not that I've ever needed a reason to pamper myself!) Beautiful décor and excellent menu. Menu includes Argentinean Kobe beef, chicken, pork, and seafood. Great breakfast buffet. Seafood is fresh with large portions.

DEL FIN DEL MUNDO

Honduras 5663, Buenos Aires, 54 11 4899-6660
www.bodegadelfindelmundo.com
CUISINE: Argentine
DRINKS: Full Bar
SERVING: Lunch, Dinner
PRICE RANGE: $$$$
NEIGHBORHOOD: Palermo
This trendy restaurant, with a lovely interior, offers five and six course meals with wine pairings. Here their specialty seems to be steak served several ways. Nice wine list.

FERVOR

Posadas 1519, Buenos Aires, 54 11 4804-4944
www.fervorbrasas.com.ar
CUISINE: Argentinian

DRINKS: Full Bar
SERVING: Lunch, Dinner
PRICE RANGE: $$
NEIGHBORHOOD: Recoleta
This trendy restaurant is a favorite of locals and tourists. Menu favorites include: Ojo de bife (rib-eye steak) and Tortilla de papas (fried potato omelet). The seafood is top-notch here as well.

FLORERÍA ATLÁNTICO
Arroyo 872, Buenos Aires, 54-11-4313-6093
www.floreriaatlantico.com.ar
CUISINE: Tapas; excellent cocktail selection
DRINKS: Full Bar
SERVING: Lunch, Dinner

PRICE RANGE: $$$
NEIGHBORHOOD: Retiro
This is a hot little place you just have to make time to
visit. Inspired by speakeasies, it hidden beneath a
flower shop. You gain entrance by passing through a
huge refrigerator door and then you move downstairs.
Though the food is top notch, you'll come here for
the creative cocktails divided on the menu by the
nationalities that inspired them: Inglaterra (for those

gin martinis), French, Italian, Polish. The
subterranean cavern is decorated with paintings of

fearsome sea monsters. As I said, the food is tasty: superior blood sausages (everybody freaks out when I eat these in the States), frogs' legs, octopus, beef tongue.

FLORIDA GARDEN
Florida 899, Buenos Aires, 54 11 4312-7902
No website
CUISINE: Coffee Shop
DRINKS: Full Bar
SERVING: Lunch, Dinner
PRICE RANGE: $
NEIGHBORHOOD: Capital Federal
This place is oozing with old-world charm. Great standup coffee bar for afternoon coffee, cookies, or pastries. A local's hangout and a favorite among the artsy set.

GRAN DABBANG
Av. Raúl Scalabrini Ortiz 1543, Buenos Aires, +54 11 4832-1186
www.grandabbang.com
WEBSITE DOWN AT PRESS TIME
CUISINE: Mediterranean/Indian
DRINKS: Beer & Wine Only
SERVING: Breakfast, Lunch & Dinner; closed Sun
PRICE RANGE: $$
NEIGHBORHOOD: Palermo
In this laid back dining room that's ultra casual with its wooden tables there's a creative menu of Mediterranean cuisine with an Asian/Indian flair. Favorites from the menu include the Burrata with

eggplant and savory pancake, quail marinated in ginger and garlic. Vegetarian options.

LA BRIGADA
Estados Unidos 465, Buenos Aires, Buenos Aires, 54 11 4361–4685
www.parrillalabrigada.com.ar
WEBSITE DOWN AT PRESS TIME
CUISINE: Steakhouse
DRINKS: Full Bar
SERVING: Lunch, Dinner
PRICE RANGE: $$$$
NEIGHBORHOOD: San Telmo
The décor is a bit elaborate mixed with soccer mementos but this is one of the best parrillas in the bohemian San Telmo area. The owner chooses his own cattle from a ranch that grass feeds them. The steaks here are so tender you can eat it with a spoon. Menu favorites include: Asado (short rib roast) and Lomo (sirloin steak, prepared with a mushroom or pepper sauce). The asado de tira especial is a delicious piece of beef with the rib bones in that weighs in at 800 grams (about 28 ounces). It's almost worth the trip to B.A. by itself.

LA CABAÑA

Av Alicia Moreau de Justo 580, Buenos Aires, 54 11 4314-3710

www.lacabana.com.ar

CUISINE: Steakhouse

DRINKS: Full Bar

SERVING: Lunch, Dinner

PRICE RANGE: $$

NEIGHBORHOOD: Puerto Madero

The third incarnation of the legendary eatery, this place specializes in beef but the menu also includes chicken, fish, and a large variety of salads. You can get pieces of beef served as large as 2.2 pounds. But I'd go for the filet mignon with noisette potatoes.

LA CABRERA

Cabrera 5099, Buenos Aires, 011 4832 5754
www.lacabrera.com.ar
CUISINE: Steakhouse
DRINKS: Full Bar
SERVING: Lunch, Dinner
PRICE RANGE: $$$$
NEIGHBORHOOD: Palermo Viejo
Housed in a former general store situated in the heart
of the nightlife district, you'll find an attractive crowd
crammed in here well after 10 P.M., stuffing
themselves before heading out for a night on the
town. This eatery offers a menu that celebrates steak.

You'll want to get the ribeye, naturally, a 3-inch cut of sheer beauty, perfectly prepared. Here the portions are large and they serve delicious sweetbreads. Side dishes include pumpkin purée and eggplant salad. Get one of the Malbecs from their extensive list that will match your steak in exquisite fashion

LA CARNICERIA

2317 Thames, Buenos Aires, +54 11 4192-0461
https://www.facebook.com/xlacarniceriax
CUISINE: Argentinean/Steakhouse
DRINKS: Beer & Wine Only
SERVING: Dinner; Open for lunch Sat & Sun
PRICE RANGE: $$
Just a couple of blocks off the Avenida Santa Fe is this casual place (butcher block tables), a favorite for meat eaters, but they do offer a fish special daily. (Don't order it—stick with the meat.) The grass-fed beef served here comes from the owner's ranch in the Pampas. Get the asado de tira (smoked short ribs). Try to grab one of the handful of seats at the bar which faces the grill. Small menu and small bar selection but they are pros at preparing and serving Argentine beef. The restaurant is small and usually packed with two seatings.

LA ESPERANZA DE LOS ASCURRA

Aguirre 526, Buenos Aires, 54 11 2058-8313
No Website
CUISINE: Tapas
DRINKS: Full Bar
SERVING: Lunch, Dinner
PRICE RANGE: $$$

NEIGHBORHOOD: Villa Crespo
This popular little tapas eatery offers a creative menu.
Menu favorites include: Prawns in garlic and Beef
testicles (mollejas). Get away from the Malbec wine
you've been drinking everywhere else and order
negronis.

LA FUERZA

Av. Dorrego 1409, Buenos Aires, +54 11 4772-4874
https://lafuerza.com.ar/
CUISINE: Pub/Argentinean
DRINKS: Full Bar
SERVING: Dinner; Lunch & Dinner on Sun
PRICE RANGE: $$$
NEIGHBORHOOD: Chacarrita
Argentinean pub offering mainly bar-type food
(tapas) and hearty main dishes. Focus on the La
Fuerza vermouth and what they're doing here is
keeping the old tradition of vermouth bars alive by a
clever reinterpretation of the theme. Be sure to try the
vermú (a traditional aperitif), available on tap in

white and red. The food more than stands up to the creative aperitifs. Try the fugazzeta (sauceless onion and cheese pizza), or go for the Milanesa con fritas a caballo (schnitzel with fries and fried eggs). Or, my absolute favorite, the Sausages.

Sausage at La Fuerza.

LA MAR, CEBICHERIA PERUANA

Arévalo 2024, Buenos Aires, +54 11 4776-5543
www.lamarcebicheria.com.ar
CUISINE: Peruvian/Seafood
DRINKS: Full Bar
SERVING: Lunch & Dinner; closed Mon
PRICE RANGE: $$
NEIGHBORHOOD: Palermo
Ceviche fans will love this elegant eatery as theirs is
top notch. Also serving fresh seafood. Reservations
recommended as this place books up fast. Nice
cocktails.

LA MEZZETTA

Avenida Alvarez Thomas 1321, Buenos Aires, +54
11 4554-7585
https://www.facebook.com/pizzeria.lamezzetta
CUISINE: Pizza/Argentinean
DRINKS: Wine & Beer
SERVING: Lunch & Dinner, Late Night
PRICE RANGE: $
NEIGHBORHOOD: Villa Ortuzar

People often ask me why there's such a fuss over
pizza in Argentina. I remind them (not that they knew
anyway) that some 60% of the population is
descended from Italians. Ergo, an intense interest in
all things involving pizza. Here you get your pizza
served quickly. Line up, order, pay, and walk to the
man cutting the pies. Pizza sold by the slice. Get the
cheese and onion fugazetta slice (after which this

joint is so justly famous) and you'll see why. Standing room only inside, a few seats outside.

LA RAMBLA
Posadas 1602, Buenos Aires, , +54 11 6679-8333
No Website
CUISINE: Sandwiches
DRINKS: No Booze
SERVING: Lunch, Dinner
PRICE RANGE: $
NEIGHBORHOOD: Capital Federal
This extremely casual café is a sandwich place offering a great variety on their menu. Menu favorites include: Perfectly cooked steak sandwich with tomato on French bread. Delivery service available.

LAS PIZARRAS
Thames 2296, Buenos Aires, +54 11 4775-0625

www.laspizarrasbistro.com
CUISINE: Argentine
DRINKS: Full bar
SERVING: Dinner; closed Mon
PRICE RANGE: $$$
NEIGHBORHOOD: Palermo
Small "closed door" restaurant so reservations are
needed. Menu favorites include: Suckling pig and
Duck confit. Great choice if you're looking for
something other than steak. Nice selection of desserts.

LO DE JOAQUIN DE ALBERDI
Jorge Luis Borges 1772, Buenos Aires, 54 11 4832-
5329
www.lodejoaquinalberdi.com/
CUISINE: Wine Bar
DRINKS: Full Bar
PRICE RANGE: $$$
NEIGHBORHOOD: Palermo
Great selection of Argentine wines served at this
popular wine bar. While you're tasting wines (and
they'll do a personalized tasting flight for you if you

like), you can snack on plates of cheese and excellent ham. A perfect place to get away from the street after a busy day of shopping.

LOS SALONES DEL PIANO NOBILE @PARK HYATT

Av. Alvear 1661, Buenos Aires, 54 11 5171-1234
https://www.hyatt.com/en-US/hotel/argentina/palacio-duhau-park-hyatt-buenos-aires/bueph/dining
CUISINE: French
DRINKS: Full Bar
SERVING: Lunch, Dinner
PRICE RANGE: $$$$
NEIGHBORHOOD: Recoleta
Located at the Palace, this lovely restaurant serves breakfast, lunch, dinner, elegant snacks and afternoon tea. Menu favorites include: Pappardelle with Veal Ragu and Lamb Burger with fried egg and arugula.

MALVON CONFITERIA

Serrano 789, Buenos Aires, 54 11 4774-2563
www.malvonba.com.ar
CUISINE: Coffee Shop/Cafeteria
DRINKS: No Booze
SERVING: Breakfast, Lunch, Dinner
PRICE RANGE: $$
NEIGHBORHOOD: Capital Federal
This popular coffee shop/cafeteria offers an ever-changing variety of foods from around the globe. They serve all day, everything from breakfast to tapas. This place is also a bakery with a variety of sweets to eat with coffee or take home. They serve an

American style brunch with pancakes and eggs
Benedict that draws huge crowds on the weekend.

MAZZO
Gurruchaga 707, Buenos Aires, 54 11 5362-3522
CUISINE: Latin American / Colombian
DRINKS: Full Bar
SERVING: Breakfast, lunch, dinner
PRICE RANGE: $$ / Cash only
NEIGHBORHOOD: Villa Crespo / Palermo Queens
In an industrial setting you sit at wooden tables or
outside. Good place in this trendy area for a quick
bite, but not much more.

MIRAMAR
Avenida San Juan 1999, Buenos Aires, 011 4304
4261
No Website
CUISINE: Argentinean/Spanish
DRINKS: Wine
SERVING: Lunch, Dinner
PRICE RANGE: $$$
NEIGHBORHOOD: El Centro

This restaurant serves typical Spanish fare. Menu offers dishes like Tortillas, Rabbita and Frog Legs. Well stocked wine cellar.

MISHIGUENE
Lafinur 3368, Buenos Aires, +54 11 5029-1979
www.mishiguene.com
CUISINE: Middle Eastern
DRINKS: Full bar
SERVING: Lunch & Dinner; Lunch only on Sun
PRICE RANGE: $$$
NEIGHBORHOOD: Palermo
It's generated a lot of buzz since it opened late in 2014. Always busy, has a great energy. It's a beautiful eatery with a menu of Middle Eastern cuisine (including some modern Jewish food, something rare in these parts) with an Argentinean twist. Dishes served are large portions perfect for sharing. Menu favorites include: Varenikes and Humas.
Impressive wine list.

NOLA
Gorriti 4389, Buenos Aires, +54 9 11 5760-6652
www.nolabuenosaires.com
CUISINE: Cajun/Creole
DRINKS: Full bar
SERVING: Dinner
PRICE RANGE: $$
NEIGHBORHOOD: Palermo
Who would have thought you'd find a gastro pub in Buenos Aires specializing in food from New Orleans?

New Orleans favorites like gumbo, buttermilk
battered fried chicken and sweetbreads are served.
Crafted beers and nice selection of wines. Very
informal dining with a "fast food" feeling.

NUCHA CAFE
Jerónimo Salguero 2587, Buenos Aires, 54 11 4802-
1615
www.nucha.com.ar
CUISINE: Argentinean/Confection Shop
DRINKS: No Booze
SERVING: Breakfast
PRICE RANGE: $
NEIGHBORHOOD: Palermo
This confection shop offers a great selection of
pastries and cakes to enjoy with coffee or tea (nice
variety). It's all made here on the premises. (They
even make their own chocolates.) Get the tortas favi,
which is layer cake with chocolate mousse & cream
crowned by a slab of light-as-air Italian meringue.
The chocolate truffles aren't bad, either.

NUESTRO SECRETO

Cerrito 1455, Buenos Aires, 54-11-4321-1552
www.fourseasons.com/buenosaires/dining/restaurants/nuestro_secreto/
CUISINE: Argentinean/BBQ
DRINKS: Full bar
SERVING: Lunch & Dinner; closed Mon & Tues
PRICE RANGE: $$$
NEIGHBORHOOD: Retiro
Located at the **Four Seasons Hotel**, this unique
eatery serves up a "backyard garden" atmosphere
complete with outdoor furniture overlooking the pool.
It's a very relaxing place, with glass walls and even a
glass roof. Cuisine is typical Argentinean with a great
selection of meats with a focus on BBQ. (But the
best choices are those cuts smoked using different
hardwoods native to the country.)

OCHO ONCE

El Salvador y Ravignani, Palermo, Buenos Aires, 15
3614-5719
www.facebook.com/ochooncemaison/#_=_
CUISINE: Steakhouse/BBQ
DRINKS: Full Bar
SERVING: Dinner – Wed – Sat
PRICE RANGE: $$$$
Like most closed door restaurants (reservations a
must) you will only find out about this place by word
of mouth. (I'm your word-of-mouth guy.) Located in
a renovated house, this small eatery offers a warm
ambiance and a delicious menu from a great chef. The
restaurant serves only organic 100% certified
Argentinian beef in a 5 course tasting menu –
changing weekly. Meats prevail but nice fish options
and delicious homemade bread. Fried cheese, quinoa
burgers, mushroom paté are among the tapas offered.
(Don't show up too early. Doesn't get busy till 11 or
even midnight.)

OSAKA

Soler 5608, Buenos Aires, 54 11 4775–6964
www.osaka.com.pe
CUISINE: Japanese Fusion
DRINKS: Full Bar
SERVING: Lunch, Dinner
PRICE RANGE: $$$$
NEIGHBORHOOD: Palermo
This innovative restaurant blends Peruvian and Asian
cuisines to the delight of their well-dressed young hip
guests who keep the place packed. Menu favorite:

Misoudado, an amazing red-curry grouper. Upstairs
and downstairs dining.

OVIEDO
Antonio Beruti 2602, Buenos Aires, 54 11 4822-5415
www.oviedoresto.com.ar
CUISINE: Argentinean/Spanish
DRINKS: Full Bar
SERVING: Lunch, Dinner
PRICE RANGE: $$$$
NEIGHBORHOOD: Capital Federal/ Recoleta
This very upscale Spanish-style restaurant offers a
menu that includes everything from classics to new
and modern creations. Excellent cheeses. Daily fish
specials are a favorite but their meats are primo as
well. Impressive wine list.

PALADAR
Camargo, Buenos Aires, +54 9 11 5797-7267
www.paladarbuenosaires.com.ar

WEBSITE DOWN AT PRESSTIME
CUISINE: Signature Cuisine (well, they said it, not me)
DRINKS: Full Bar
SERVING: Dinner & Late Night
PRICE RANGE: $$$$
With quite a few options to the "closed door" scene in Buenos Aires, this is a lovely choice where reservations are made online and they send you the address. Creative menu is most filled with traditional but innovative Argentinian dishes. The owners speak English and welcome all for a lovely dining experience.

PARRILLA DON JULIO
Guatemala 4691, Buenos Aires, +54 11 4831-9564
www.parrilladonjulio.com.ar
CUISINE: Steakhouse
DRINKS: Full Bar
SERVING: Lunch & Dinner
PRICE RANGE: $$
NEIGHBORHOOD: Palermo
Popular steakhouse serving classic steaks and local dishes. Menu picks: Rib Eye (from grass-fed cattle) and Flan (for dessert). Upscale dining with perfect service – don't go here if you're in a rush. Nice wine selection.

PATAGONIA SUR

Rocha 801, Buenos Aires, 54 11 4303-5917
www.restaurantepatagoniasur.com
CUISINE: Argentinean
DRINKS: Full Bar
SERVING: Lunch, Dinner
PRICE RANGE: $$$$
NEIGHBORHOOD: Boca/Capital Federal
Run by Francis Mallman, chef and author, who offers
an impressive menu of Argentinean fare that
showcases local produce. Menu favorites include: 7
hour Lamb and Beef tenderloin with bacon. Very
impressive wine cellar. Reservations necessary.

RODI BAR

Vincente Lopez 1900, Buenos Aires, +54 11 4801-
5230
No Website
CUISINE: Peruvian
DRINKS: Beer & Wine Only

SERVING: Lunch & Dinner; closed Sun
PRICE RANGE: $$$
NEIGHBORHOOD: Recoleta
Intimate (yes, the tables are that close together) high-end eatery with a loyal following. This place has long been an institution in the wealthy Recoleta district, but the food is simple and unpretentious. A good place to get a cheap combination plate. Menu favorites include: Veal cutlet with fried egg and Spinach crepes. Reservations recommended.

SACRO

Costa Rica 6038, Buenos Aires, +54 11 3984-0059
http://www.sacro.com.ar/
CUISINE: Healthy/Vegetarian Friendly/Vegan
Options
DRINKS: Wine & Beer
SERVING: Lunch & Dinner
PRICE RANGE: $$$$
NEIGHBORHOOD: Palermo

Upscale health eatery offering a menu that emphasizes gourmet vegan/vegetarian dishes in a modern setting, but they do have some meat on the menu, so never fear. The outside setting is really pleasant. Favorites: Almond ricotta gnudi; Jackfruit bao; Avocado key lime pie; Spaghetti Asiático and Nachos. Reservations recommended.

SALGADO ALIMENTOS
Juan Ramírez de Velazco 401, Buenos Aires, 54 11 4854-1336
www.salgadoalimentos.com.ar/
WEBSITE DOWN AT PRESS TIME
CUISINE: Italian/Pasta
DRINKS: Full Bar
SERVING: Lunch, Dinner
PRICE RANGE: $
NEIGHBORHOOD: Villa Crespo / Palermo Queens
This popular Italian eatery offers a menu with a variety of homemade pastas and sauces. Unlike some

of the trendier new arrivals to this recently hot area,
this place has been around for many years. Try the
Pumpkin Ravioli or the pork shoulder ravioli. An old
favorite here is the "provoleta," or grilled provolone.
Just add a little salt and you're in heaven. Outdoor
seating. Delivery available.

SALVAJE BAKERY
Av. Dorrego 1829, Buenos Aires, +54 11 2474-3573
www.salvajebakery.com.ar
CUISINE: Italian/Fusion
DRINKS: No Booze
SERVING: Breakfast, Lunch & Dinner; Closed Mon

PRICE RANGE: $
NEIGHBORHOOD: Palermo
Café-style eatery. Begin your day like most locals
with a Medialuna (a kind of sweet croissant),
toast with cream cheese and jam, and coffee,
coffee, coffee. Always there's rich smelling
coffee. Besides these essentials, they offer
gourmet baked goods, light eats, and brunch. Pastries
and breads available to go. Only a handulf of tables,
so come early or plan to take out your order.

STRANGE BREWING
Delgado 658, C1Buenos Aires, +54 11 2627-4840
https://strange.com.ar/
CUISINE: Beer Bar

DRINKS: Beer & Wine
SERVING: Dinner; Closed Mon & Tues
PRICE RANGE: $$
NEIGHBORHOOD: Colegiales
Microbrewery offering a menu of (mostly) healthy fare, breads, cheeses, cakes, and sandwiches. Impressive beer selection offering 10 brews served on a rotating basis including an IPA, pale ale, amber, and dunkel & others. Very tasty bites come from the kitchen, my favorites being the succulent empanadas, an osso buco grilled cheese that is so rich you think you'll faint, and perhaps the biggest (and highest) plate of nachos I've ever seen. Really nice buzz in this place.

SUNAE ASIAN CANTINA

Humboldt 1626, Buenos Aires, +54 11 4776-8122
https://cantinasunae.com/
CUISINE: Thai/Filipino/Vietnamese
DRINKS: Full Bar
SERVING: Dinner; Closed Sun
PRICE RANGE: $$$
NEIGHBORHOOD: Palermo
Café offering a healthy menu of Asian inspired cuisine. Favorites: Sio Mai (comes with pork dumplings) and Khao Soi (chicken with egg noodles). Delicious curry dishes. Unique desserts like the Carioca Pop (rice balls with fruit and purple potato ice cream).

TEGUI

Costa Rica 5852, Buenos Aires, 54 11 4770 9500
www.tegui.com.ar

CUISINE: Eclectic
DRINKS: Full Bar
SERVING: Lunch, Dinner
PRICE RANGE: $$$$
NEIGHBORHOOD: Palermo
Local culinary bigwig German Martitegue opened

Tegui in 2009 and has been serving crowds ever
since. Very stylish eatery with an open-air kitchen in
the rear. (You go through a large display of wine
bottles up front, then pass through an atrium with
palm trees, before getting to the rear.) Very handsome
staff, right out of some modeling agency. The menu is
prix-fixe with four choices for starters, entrees, and
desserts. Menu favorites include: Cow-brain pie with
prosciutto and shallot cream sauce and Rabbit-stuffed
ravioli. But menu changes every week. Extensive
wine list. I'd advise reservations. Restaurant

magazine dubbed this the 9th best restaurant among the top 50 in all of Latin America.

TOMO 1

Carlos Pellegrini 521, Buenos Aires, +54 11 4326 6698

www.tomo1.com.ar

CUISINE: Argentine / Spanish / Italian

DRINKS: Full bar

SERVING: Lunch & Dinner; closed Sun

PRICE RANGE: $$$$

NEIGHBORHOOD: San Nicolas

Located in the **Panamericano Buenos Aires Hotel & Resort**, this is a formal upscale eatery with white tablecloths and exquisite service to match. A good idea here is to get the 3-course tasting menu. Price includes 2 glasses of wine, coffee and dessert, so in a place like this, it's a bargain. . Menu favorites include: Patagonia lamb gigot and the delicious dessert crème brûlée trio (combination of vanilla, dulce de leche and coffee). Reservations recommended.

NIGHTLIFE

BEBOP CLUB
Moreno 364, Buenos Aires, +54 11 4331-3409
www.bebopclub.com.ar
NEIGHBORHHOOD: Monserrat
Reminiscent of a swanky New York jazz club.
Downstairs is the club; upstairs is a nice restaurant
with an extensive wine list, **Aldo's Restoran
Vinoteca**. There's a drink minimum in the club
portion. Jazz & Blues. International as well as local
music acts featured. Closed Mondays.

THE HARRISON SPEAKEASY
Palermo Soho
C1414DMJ, Malabia 1764, Buenos Aires, 54 11 4831 0519
http://www.nickynysushi.com/
The "closed door" concept is popular in Buenos Aires and they have many "speakeasy" themed bars. To gain entrance to this bar you need to have friends that have a membership card or have dinner at **Nicky's NY** sushi bar and when you finish dinner ask to visit the wine cellar. You'll be sent through a door in the rear of the place that looks like a vault. Once inside, it's a great bar scene and it really feels like you're in a New York bar in the 1920s, with the big wooden bar and the sparkling crystal chandeliers.

ISABEL BAR
Uriarte 1664 Ciudad Autonoma, Buenos Aires, 54-11 4834-6969
www.isabelbar.com
NEIGHBORHOOD: Palermo Soho

Open since 2010, this trendy bar became famous as the place to spot models. Drinks are purchased with Isabelitas, 25-peso poker chips purchased upon entering the club. The bar has a funky classic décor with an outside patio.

LA CATEDRAL
Sarmiento 4006, Buenos Aires, 54 11 5325 1630
www.lacatedralclub.com/
NEIGHBORHOOD: Almagro
This underground club is a mixture of post-punk/neo-goth and circus/music hall. Great tango experience for watching and learning the dance. The regulars here often invite strangers to dance the tango, so you can learn a few steps. Cover charge.

LA PLAYITA
Roseti 722, Buenos Aires
www.agrupacionlaplayita.blogspot.com.ar
NEIGHBORHOOD: Chacarita

You have to ring a doorbell to get into this old reconditioned house that sports a patio and bar where concerts are put on by a variety of performers. On busy nights, a line forms. You pay a cheap cover and then you're in a world of cast-off sofas, mismatched chairs, cheap local beers that are cold and delicious and a underground scene.

LA TRASTIENDA CLUB
Balcarce 460 San Telmo, Buenos Aires, 54 11 4342-5162
www.latrastienda.com
NEIGHBORHOOD: San Telmo
Translated as The Hidden, this club is located in the historic district in a building that was once an old general store. This place is a landmark in the cultural scene of the city. Here all styles of music are performed including Pop, Rock, Reggae, Electronic, World, Tango, Jazz and Folklore.

LA VIRUTA

Armenia 1366, Buenos Aires, +54 11 4775-0160
https://lavirutatangoclub.com/
NEIGHBORHOOD: Palermo Soho
One of the most popular dance venues in Buenos
Aires that is also know for the dance classes
scheduled every day and night. If you pay once, you
can attend as many classes as you want during that
day. Tango rules here and the slippery dance floor is
ideal. Tables are available if you just want to drink
and watch (which is where I personally fit in). Live
music. This place gets packed around 3 a.m. and is
open until dawn. (How these people do it, I don't
know. You and old, they're all up late.)

TEATRO COLÓN

Cerrito 628, Buenos Aires, 54 11 4378-7100
www.teatrocolon.org.ar
NEIGHBORHOOD: Capital Federal
Open since 1908, this is the main opera house in the
city and the third best opera house in the world
(according to National Geographic). After a
refurbishment the venue reopened in 2010.

TORQUATO TASSO

Defensa 1575 San Telmo, Buenos Aires, 54 4307
6506
www.torquatotasso.com.ar
NEIGHBORHOOD: Capital Federal
This is one of the city's best live-music venues and
especially a great place to hear live tango music.
Popular bands that regularly play here include:
Orchestra Típica Leopoldo Federico, Sexteto Mayor
and La Chicana. Cover charge.

VERNE COCKTAIL CLUB

Av. Medrano 1475, Buenos Aires, +54 11 4822-0980
www.vernecocktailclub.com
NEIGHBORHHOOD: Palermo
This place stands out among the other "speakeasy"
style bars in Buenos Aires. This offers the most
authentic speakeasy experience. Reservations
recommended. Try the Opium Old Fashioned (made

with Jim Beam) – it's a winner but all the cocktails
are top notch.

VICTORIA BROWN

Costa Rica 4827, Buenos Aires, 54 11 4831-0831
www.victoriabrownbar.com
WEBSITE DOWN AT PRESSTIME
NEIGHBORHOOD: Palermo
In jaded upscale Palermo, this place has got people
buzzing like schoolchildren. In the daytime, it's
known for putting out a superior brunch menu. But
when the sun goes down, the phony brick wall slides
open revealing a plush speakeasy bar entered through
a secret passage. The craft cocktails really involve
some craft. The Desde Cuba con Amor comes out
literally smoking. Once you're inside, the mood is
friendly. Interesting bar menu featuring treats like
octopus and spicy French toast.